America, My Country
Native Peoples

The Kwakiutl

By Doraine Bennett

Content Review, With Special Thanks
Deidre Cullon, Ph.D. Candidate
Consulting Anthropologist
University of Victoria
Victoria, British Columbia, Canada

STATE
STANDARDS
PUBLISHING ®

Your State • Your Standards • Your Grade Level

Dear Educators, Librarians and Parents . . .

Thank you for choosing books from State Standards Publishing! This book supports state Departments of Educations' standards for elementary level social studies and has been measured by the ATOS Readability Formula for Books (Accelerated Reader), the Lexile Framework for Reading, and the Fountas & Pinnell Benchmark Assessment System for Guided Reading. Photographs and/or illustrations, captions, and other design elements have been included to provide supportive visual messaging to enhance text comprehension. Glossary and Word Index sections introduce key new words and help young readers develop skills in locating and combining information. "Think With Bagster" questions provide teachers and parents with tools for additional learning activities and critical thinking development. We wish you all success in using this book to meet your student or child's learning needs.

Jill Ward, President

Publisher

State Standards Publishing, LLC
1788 Quail Hollow
Hamilton, GA 31811, USA
1.866.740.3056, www.statestandardspublishing.com

Cataloging-in-Publication Data

Bennett, Doraine.
  The Kwakiutl / Doraine Bennett.
    p. cm. -- (America, my country Native Peoples)
  Includes index.
  ISBN 978-1-935884-90-3 (lib. bdg.)
  ISBN 978-1-935884-96-5 (pbk.)
  1. Kwakiutl Indians--Juvenile literature.   I. Title.
  979.5--dc23

                    2012948404

About the Author

Doraine Bennett has a degree in professional writing from Columbus State University in Columbus, Georgia, and has been writing and teaching writing for over twenty years. She is a published author of numerous books for children, as well as magazine articles for both children and adults. She is the editor of the National Infantry Association's *Infantry Bugler* magazine. Doraine enjoys reading and flower gardening. She lives in Georgia with her husband, Cliff.

Editor's Note:

The style of the boat prows depicted on pages 4 and 23, as interpreted by noted American artist W. Langdon Kihn, is more ornate than would typically be crafted by the Kwakiutl. Similarly, the totem poles depicted on these pages, by the same artist, are consistent with the style used in a northwest coast village that would have been located north of the Kwakiutl.

1 2 3 4 5 – CG – 17 16 15 14 13

Table of Contents

Hi, I'm Bagster! Let's learn about Native Peoples.

The Pacific Ocean with its bays and inlets was the center of Kwakiutl community life.

Saying Hello

If you had been a Kwakiutl boy long ago, you might have spent the day helping your father catch salmon. A Kwakiutl girl would have helped her mother pack dried salmon into cedar boxes to store for winter food. If you wanted to know how many salmon you had caught or packed, you would count. *'Nam, ma'l, yudaxwa, mu, sak'a* (nam, mall, u-dax-wuh, moo, sa-kah). One, two, three, four, five.

The Kwakiutl native language is called Kwak'wala. If you wanted to say hello or thank you to this girl or boy, you would say *gilakasla*. It sounds a little like gee-lah-kah-slah. Pronounce the "g" the way it sounds in go.

The Kwakiutl are Native Americans of the Pacific Northwest. Scientists called **archaeologists** have found evidence that Kwakiutl people may have lived in this area for at least 8,000 years. The Pacific Ocean with its bays and inlets was the center of their community life, and still is today.

At Home along the Coast

Long ago, the Kwakiutl lived on Vancouver Island and the mainland of British Columbia, Canada, directly opposite the island. The rocky shores here were steep and covered with dense, evergreen forests. Deep fjords pushed into the mainland. A **fjord** (fee-ord) is an ocean inlet between high cliffs. There were many smaller islands in the fjords and off the mainland coast. The Kwakiutl could easily navigate, or travel through, the channels by canoe. Most Kwakiutl villages were established near the mouth of a river where the land was level enough to build.

Vancouver Island is nearly 200 miles long. It sheltered the Kwakiutl lands when storms blew in from the ocean.

A fjord is an ocean inlet between high cliffs.

How did the land and water shape the Kwakiutl way of life?

MY STATE

Most Kwakiutl villages were established near the mouth of a river where the land was level enough to build.

Monkeys like this spider monkey swing through thick treetops in tropical rain forests.

Decribe the two types of rain forests. What effect does location have on these?

Animals like the Roosevelt Elk graze on grasses and plants that grow well in the wet, cool climate of temperate rain forests.

In the Rain Forest

This area of the Pacific Northwest coast has the largest **temperate** rain forest on earth. Have you studied tropical rain forests near the equator? Tropical rain forests are wet and hot. Temperate rain forests are located farther away from the equator. They are usually wet and cool. Not many temperate rain forests exist. An ocean with warm currents and mountains near the coast must be present for the forest to form. Near Canada, moist air blows in from the Pacific Ocean, causing rain, fog, and mist nearly all year. The Coast Mountains trap the moisture and keep it from moving inland. Dense forests grow in this moist climate. Summers are cool and winters are very wet and mild, which makes growing crops difficult.

Long ago, each Kwakiutl family had its own territory. During the warm months, the Kwakiutl roamed their land freely. They used several sites as temporary homes. They hunted, fished, and collected food while the weather was good. When winter came, all the families moved to a permanent place where they held feasts and conducted religious ceremonies.

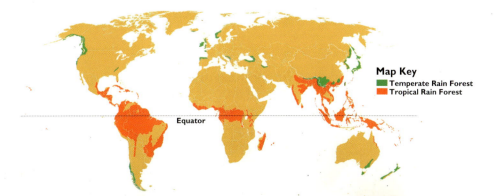

Map Key
- Temperate Rain Forest
- Tropical Rain Forest

Equator

Being Resourceful

The Pacific Northwest is rich in **natural resources**. Large forests provided wood for building. Freshwater rivers and streams gave the Kwakiutl water to drink. They fished in the ocean and hunted in the forests. The Kwakiutl people worked with natural resources to produce goods or services. They were **human resources**.

Because the Kwakiutl did not depend on growing crops as their main food source, they mostly lived as hunters, gatherers, and fishers. Most hunter-gatherer tribes moved from place to place looking for food. But the Kwakiutl learned to use their natural resources wisely. These resources, especially the abundance of salmon, allowed them to stay in one area. They built homes, crafted canoes, and carved **totem poles** with wood from the forests. They made blankets from the skins of beavers, sea otters, and fur seals. They used the intestines of whales and sea lions to make bags and strings for their bows. They made a thick, buttery oil from the tiny eulachon, or candlefish. They made containers for the oil from bull kelp, a type of seaweed. These goods made by people are called **capital resources**.

Natural Resource	Human Resource	Capital Resource
Red cedar tree	Kwakiutl man	Canoe
Eulachon	Kwakiutl woman	Oil
Bull kelp	Kwakiutl girl	Bottle
Stone	Kwakiutl boy	Arrowhead

The abundance of salmon allowed the Kwakiutl to stay in one area, unlike most hunter-gatherer peoples.

11

| Halibut | Herring | Salmon |

The Kwakiutl built fences on the streams to catch salmon, like this weir built by the Cowichan (cow-itch-en) Indians, who lived on southern Vancouver Island.

Hunting and Fishing

Early in the spring, Kwakiutl men caught herring with a type of rake. They caught giant halibut with fishing lines made from bull kelp. Halibut hooks were often made of wood from yew and hemlock trees.   To catch salmon, they built a fence of poles, called a **weir**, across the stream. The fences trapped the fish as they swam upriver to their spawning grounds, where fish lay their eggs.

Groups of hunters paddled canoes in search of sea otters, sea lions, and seals. They used wooden **harpoons** to kill these **marine mammals**.

The men hunted Canada geese at night from canoes, using a small fire to help them hide. At first, a small mat was held over the fire to hide the flames, then removed several times so the geese would get accustomed to the light but would not see the hunters. After awhile, the hunters would paddle toward the geese, hiding behind the mat and flames, and throw a framed net on top of the birds to catch them.

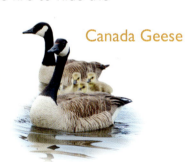

Canada Geese

The halibut is a flatfish that lives mostly on the sea floor in shallow waters. The halibut has some unusual features. It covers itself in sand and uses **camouflage** as a form of disguise to look like its surroundings. This protects the halibut from predators but also makes it very hard for fishermen to spot. Like other bottom-dwelling fish, both of the halibut's eyes are on its topside, allowing it to see as it lies on the ocean floor. Halibut can reach up to eight feet long or more and weigh hundreds of pounds.

Food and Medicine from Nature

Women collected clams and other shellfish from the shallow waters of the shore. To increase the clam harvest, they removed the rocks from the beaches to create a **clam garden**. In summer and fall, they gathered elderberries, blackberries, and red huckleberries, which were plentiful in the forests. Crabapple and wild cherry trees provided delicious fruit each season. Edible roots and leaves added variety to meals. In summer, the Kwakiutl grilled or baked their fish and meat. Fish were dried and stored in wooden boxes for winter.

The Kwakiutl used many native plants as medicine. They used rockweed, a type of seaweed, to treat sores, swollen feet, and pain in the legs. They wore deerskin gloves to collect devil's club, a bushy plant with sharp spines. They thought the spines had magical powers to protect against evil. Sucking on a piece of devil's club root cured stomach pains. The raven, a black bird,

was believed to have supernatural powers. If a child was sick, they placed a raven under its head or on its chest to prevent the child from dying.

The Dungeness (dun-juh-ness) crab was an important Kwakiutl food source, and still is today. They boiled the crabs and ate the delicious white meat. Some Kwakiutl ate the orange eggs, called salmonberries, inside the female crab. The Dungeness crab has become a popular seafood delicacy enjoyed by people all over the world.

Women collected clams and other shellfish from the shallow waters of the shore.

The Kwakiutl dried fish and stored them in wooden boxes for winter.

Wealthy Kwakiutl wore button blankets.

Waterproof capes made of cedar bark kept the Kwakiutl dry during the rains.

Getting Dressed

Kwakiutl women made all of the clothing. Most clothing was woven from the fibers of cedar tree bark. This made a kind of waterproof cloth that gave protection from the frequent rains. In the warmer months, men often wore no clothes at all in the gentle climate. Women wore cedar bark aprons or skirts.

In cooler weather, women added a cone-shaped cape around the shoulders. For extra warmth, both men and women added a bark robe draped around the shoulders. The robe was sometimes trimmed with fur to soften the edges or woven with strips of sea otter fur. Chiefs and wealthy Kwakiutl sometimes wore robes made from the fur of sea otters, bears, or even mink. Waterproof hats, woven from cedar bark or spruce tree roots, kept the head dry. The Kwakiutl wore moccasins only in winter.

Women often wore their hair in two braids. Men usually wore their hair loose or tied at the neck. Men sometimes grew mustaches and beards. Wealthy or important Kwakiutl wore earrings and nose rings made from bones and shells.

The Kwakiutl dressed differently for their celebrations and feasts. They wore decorated cloaks and leggings. Wealthy Kwakiutl wore button blankets. These finely woven blankets were decorated with buttons sewn in fancy designs. The buttons were made from the insides of sea shells.

17

The Potlatch

The Kwakiutl lived in a class society. They believed some people were born into the upper classes, much like European royalty. These people were born with the right to certain names, songs, and dances. They kept that right all their lives. They displayed their rank by holding a **potlatch**, a special gift-giving ceremony. Potlatches were also held to celebrate accomplishments, to give names, or to mourn, or remember, someone who had died. A successful potlatch might take several years to plan and could last for several days.

The Kwakiutl believed they gained great honor by giving away their possessions. The more they gave away, the more honor they brought to themselves. At the potlatch, the host gave gifts to invited guests from other family groups. The host gave away blankets, baskets, and mats. He gave away canoes and other valuable or useful items. When guests accepted gifts, they agreed to recognize their host's class ranking or special right. The host was expected to offer more food than his guests could eat. He didn't worry if he gave away everything he owned.

The Kwakiutl believed that one creature could change into another. They recreated these changes with **transformation masks** that had moving parts. The wearer began as one creature, then changed, or transformed, into another creature by pulling hidden strings to open and close the mask.

A potlatch was held to honor a birth, a marriage, or a death. It was also a way to display a person's class in Kwakiutl society.

19

Several families lived together in the home.

Homes were often painted like a large animal representing the family and its history.

Making a Home Together

The Kwakiutl lived in large rectangular homes made from cedar planks. Red cedar trees were best for building. The wood did not decay easily, even in the rainy climate. It was lightweight, but strong. The Kwakiutl carved images on the beams inside their homes and on totem poles outside. The carvings represented animals, people, and spirit beings important to the family and its history.

The front of the house was often painted like a large animal representing the family group. The door was painted to look like the mouth of the creature.

Several related families lived together in the home. Families lived along the sides of the building. A plank wall or blanket separated the families. The back wall was used by those from the upper classes. The center of the room held a shared fireplace. Planks of the roof were lifted to allow smoke to escape.

Bull kelp is a large type of seaweed with very long, hollow stems. Sometimes the Kwakiutl buried the stems beneath the floors of houses. At potlatch time, everything was moved out of the house to make room for guests. When performers danced around the fireplace, the hollow kelp stems made sounds that seemed to come from the fire.

Creative Minds

The Kwakiutl were excellent craftsmen. Much of the time in their winter villages was spent working on their crafts. They used simple tools, but their canoes, masks, and totem poles were beautiful works of art. A tree trunk for a canoe would be burned out, steamed, shaped, and polished. The burning caused the wood to harden. Then the canoe was often carved and painted with special designs. Totem poles carved with family symbols told about the history of families or communities. Sometimes they told stories about journeys to other worlds or other important events. Totem poles could also be a symbol of a family's power or rank.

Many useful, everyday items were carved and painted, too. The Kwakiutl made **kerfed**, waterproof boxes from a single piece of wood. The craftsman made three cuts across a cedar plank. The cuts stopped just short of going all the way through the wood. He filled a pit with water and hot rocks, placed the plank over it, and covered it to keep in the steam. When the wood was soft, the craftsman bent it at the cuts. He joined the edges together with pegs. Another plank was attached to the bottom with wooden pegs. The box was made so well it would hold water or oil.

Kerfed boxes like this would hold water or oil.

The canoe was carved and painted with special designs.

How do you think the Kwakiutl spent some of their time? What does this tell you about their society?

The Kwakiutl were excellent craftsmen. Their canoes, masks, and totem poles were beautiful works of art.

23

The Kwakiutl traded for iron, copper, tools, and guns.

European fur traders were the first white people the Kwakiutl saw.

Trading with Europeans

European explorers and fur traders were the first white people the Kwakiutl saw. Captain James Cook, an English explorer, arrived at Vancouver Island in 1778. Although his ship docked south of Kwakiutl land, hundreds of Indians went to see his ship. Some of the Kwakiutl were probably among the curious Indians.

In 1792, George Vancouver, who was captain of a British ship from England, visited Namgis (num-gees) Indian villages near the Kwakiutl. The Indians held a greeting ceremony to welcome the men. Soon the Kwakiutl began trading with the newcomers. At first the Kwakiutl traded sea otter skins for beads, buttons, and other trinkets. But they were good traders. Soon they traded for iron, copper, tools, and guns. They traded for cloth, mirrors, and cooking pots. They also bargained for flour and rice, tea and sugar.

Kwakiutl people witnessed European customs from the white traders. Missionaries, a type of priest, came to teach them about the Christian religion. The Kwakiutl argued over these new ways.

Trading was fierce. Many tribes wanted to trade with the British and American traders. Battles broke out among the tribes trying to capture skins. Many sea otters were killed for trading. Before long, the sea otter population grew smaller and smaller.

Coal, Conflict, and Change

In the 1800s, coal was discovered on Kwakiutl land. The Kwakiutl mined the coal and sold it to the Hudson's Bay Company, a trading company that operated in other parts of Canada. In 1849, the company brought in its own men to mine the coal. They built a fort and trading post, called Fort Rupert. More and more Kwakiutl moved to be near the trading post. The whites and the Indians argued over who owned the coal. Many fights took place. Mining at Fort Rupert did not last long, because the Hudson's Bay Company found better quality coal nearby. The trading post stayed open until 1873.

In the late 1880s, the Canadian government took native Kwakiutl land and set aside **reserves**, or plots of land, to be used by the Kwakiutl. Sometimes they took back parts of the reserves they had promised. One policy said an Indian could not own more than ten acres of land, but a white man could own 200 acres. The Kwakiutl no longer had enough land to hunt and fish. They had to work for white people to make a living.

The government made other changes, too. The potlatch was outlawed. Government officials thought that giving away possessions was wasteful. They wanted the Kwakiutl to follow Canadian laws and customs. Schools would not allow children to speak Kwak'wala. The Kwakiutl were not allowed to vote. Many of their totem poles were torn down or left to rot in the moist, rainy weather.

How did life change for the Kwakiutl?

Many totem poles were torn down or left to rot in the moist, rainy weather.

Salmon Fishing

Potlatch Today

Raising Totem Pole

The Kwakiutl Today

Today, the Kwakiutl consider themselves to be part of a group called Kwakwaka'wakw (kwah-kwu-kyu-wah-kwuh). These are all the people who speak the language Kwak'wala. The Kwakiutl are those from the village of Fort Rupert. Those in other villages have different names.

The Canadian government finally changed the way it treated the Kwakiutl. The government provided better health care and education. The Kwakiutl tribe is governed by an internal council. Today's Kwakiutl are also Canadian citizens and obey Canadian laws.

Most Kwakiutl children speak English as their first language. Many schools have programs that teach Kwak'wala, as well as native arts and crafts. Most Kwakiutl wear modern clothes, but many still wear the basket hat and other traditional **regalia** during ceremonies. They once again celebrate the potlatch on special occasions. They still raise totem poles. They keep their culture alive through traditional songs, dances, and stories.

Painted House at Museum

29

Glossary

archaeologists – Scientists who learn about past human life by studying objects left by ancient people.

camouflage – A way to disguise or hide something by covering it up or making it harder to see, such as using markings or color to blend with the surroundings.

capital resources – Goods produced and used to make other goods and services.

clam garden – A beach structure used to increase clam harvest, created by building a rock wall at low tide that would fill in with sand and expand butter clam habitat.

fjord – A long, narrow inlet of the ocean between high cliffs.

harpoons – Spears used for hunting whales and large fish.

human resources – People working to produce goods and services.

kerfed – Wood that has been cut with grooves, or notches, by a saw or other cutting tool.

marine mammals – Mammals living in the sea. Mammals are warm-blooded animals with backbones that feed their young with milk.

natural resources – Things that come directly from nature that are useful to humans.

potlatch – A gift-giving ceremony to confirm rights, give names, or mourn the dead.

regalia – Special clothing and ornaments worn for ceremonies and special occasions.

reserve – An area of land set aside by the Canadian government for the use of native peoples. Called a reservation in the United States.

temperate – Having neither very hot nor very cold temperatures, and mild weather.

totem pole – A pole carved and painted with animals, plants, and other natural objects to represent a family or clan, or to tell of an important event.

transformation masks – Ceremonial masks that use moving parts to change from one creature or face to another.

weir – A fence-like or basket-like trap used to catch fish.

Index

Editorial and Image Credits

Designer: Michael Sellner, Corporate Graphics, North Mankato, Minnesota
Consultant/Marketing Design: Alison Hagler, Basset and Becker Advertising, Columbus, Georgia

Images © copyright contributor unless otherwise specified.
Cover – "Native Americans Arrive for Potlatch" by W. Langdon Kihn. **4/5** – See Cover. **6/7** – Village: "Indians of the Northwest Coast"/ Milwaukee Public Museum; Fjord: Frédéric de Goldschmidt/Wikipedia; Map: Qyd/Wikipedia. **8/9** – Elk: Natalia Bratslavsky/iStockphoto; Monkey: Worlds Wildlife Wonders/ShutterStock; Map: Karl Udo Gerth/Wikipedia. **10/11** – Canoe: North Wind Picture Archives. **12/13** – Weir: Frederick Dally/National Archives of Canada/C-65097; Halibut: Magnus Kjaergaard/Wikipedia; Herring: AlaskaStock/Alamy; Salmon: Ihoe/iStockphoto; Geese: Digital Paws Inc/iStockphoto. **14/15** – Village: "Sara's Ridge" by Martin Pate/pateart.com; Woman: NativeStock; Chef: Digital Paws Inc/iStockphoto. **16/17** – Man & Woman: NativeStock; Headdress: "Raven Headdress" by W. Langdon Kihn. **18/19** – Potlatch: Joanna Simpson Wilson/National Archives of Canada/C-74714; Mask: The Art Gallery Collection/Alamy. **20/21** – Village: "Kwakiutl Village on Gilford Island" by Erkki (Eric) Nevatie/quartermasterdesign.com; Interior: John Webber/National Archives of Canada/C-3676; Kelp: Deb Gleason/iStockphoto. **22/23** – Totem: "Native Americans Raising a Totem Pole" by W. Langdon Kihn; Canoe: "Native Americans Decorating a Canoe" by W. Langdon Kihn; Box: NativeStock. **24/25** – Ship: North Wind Picture Archives; Traders – "Native Canadians Bartering Furs" by William Ralston; Otter: US Fish & Wildlife Service/Wikipedia. **26/27** – Images AA-00007 & AA00089 courtesy of Royal British Columbia Museum, BC Archives. **28/29** – Fishing: Ted Spiegel/CORBIS; Potlatch: Frans Lanting Studio/Alamy; Totem: Lawrence Migdale PIX/Alamy; House: Ryan Bushby/Wikipedia.

Think With Bagster

1. Look at the map on page 9. How are temperate rain forests different from tropical rain forests? How are they alike?

2. Look at the chart on page 10. Can you think of other natural resources the Kwakiutl used? What are some other capital resources they produced? Pick a natural resource that is used today. Explain how it is used by human resources to become a capital resource.

3. Read this Kwakiutl greeting:

   "We are the Kwakiutl. We have lived here, on the northeastern shores of Vancouver Island, since time immemorial. Our ancestors hunted and fished on these lands and waters, and developed a rich culture through which they celebrated the diversity of life around them. We continue to be strong by honouring all that our ancestors have taught us."

   What do you think the Kwakiutls' ancestors taught them? Can you think of things and ideas you have that came from your ancestors?

4. Why do you think some Kwakiutl chose to adopt white ways? Why might others not like the influence of white settlers? How could these different opinions cause trouble in the Kwakiutl tribe?

5. What was the importance of salmon to the Kwakiutl long ago? How did this resource affect the way they lived then? How does this resource affect the way they live today?

Read all the books in this series!

GRL/DRA: RS/40

ISBN 978-1-935884-96-5

90000

9 781935 884965

STATE STANDARDS PUBLISHING

Your State • Your Standards • Your Grade Level

statestandardspublishing.com

$2.50

NASCAR RACERS

ROAD THUNDER